This book is due for return on or before the last date shown
above: it may, subject to the book not being reserved by
another reader, be renewed by personal application, post, or
telephone, quoting this date and details of the book.

HAMPSHIRE COUNTY COUNCIL
County Library

100% recycled paper

UNFORGETTABLE...

PIANO SOLOS

The Lighter Side of Jazz

Wise Publications
London / New York / Paris / Sydney / Copenhagen / Madrid

Exclusive Distributors:
Music Sales Limited
8/9 Frith Street,
London W1V 5TZ, England.
Music Sales Pty Limited
120 Rothschild Avenue,
Rosebery, NSW 2018,
Australia.

Order No. AM950774
ISBN 0-7119-7053-X
This book © Copyright 1998 by Wise Publications

Music compiled by Peter Evans
Book design by Pearce Marchbank, Studio Twenty, London
Computer layout by Ben May
Cover photograph courtesy of Telegraph Colour Library

Printed in the United Kingdom by
Redwood Books Limited, Trowbridge, Wiltshire.

Your Guarantee of Quality
As publishers, we strive to produce every book to the highest
commercial standards. This book has been carefully designed to
minimise awkward page turns and to make playing from it a real
pleasure. Particular care has been given to specifying acid-free,
neutral-sized paper made from pulps which have not been
elemental chlorine bleached. This pulp is from farmed sustainable
forests and was produced with special regard for the environment.
Throughout, the printing and binding have been planned to ensure a
sturdy, attractive publication which should give years of enjoyment.
If your copy fails to meet our high standards, please inform us
and we will gladly replace it.

Music Sales' complete catalogue describes thousands of titles
and is available in full colour sections by subject, direct from
Music Sales Limited. Please state your areas of interest and
send a cheque/postal order for £1.50 for postage to:
Music Sales Limited, Newmarket Road,
Bury St. Edmunds, Suffolk IP33 3YB.

Visit the Internet Music Shop at
http://www.musicsales.co.uk

Caravan

By Duke Ellington, Irving Mills & Juan Tizol

Chelsea Bridge

By Billy Strayhorn

Don't Get Around Much Anymore

Words by Bob Russell
Music by Duke Ellington

12

Early Autumn

Words by Johnny Mercer
Music by Ralph Burns & Woody Herman

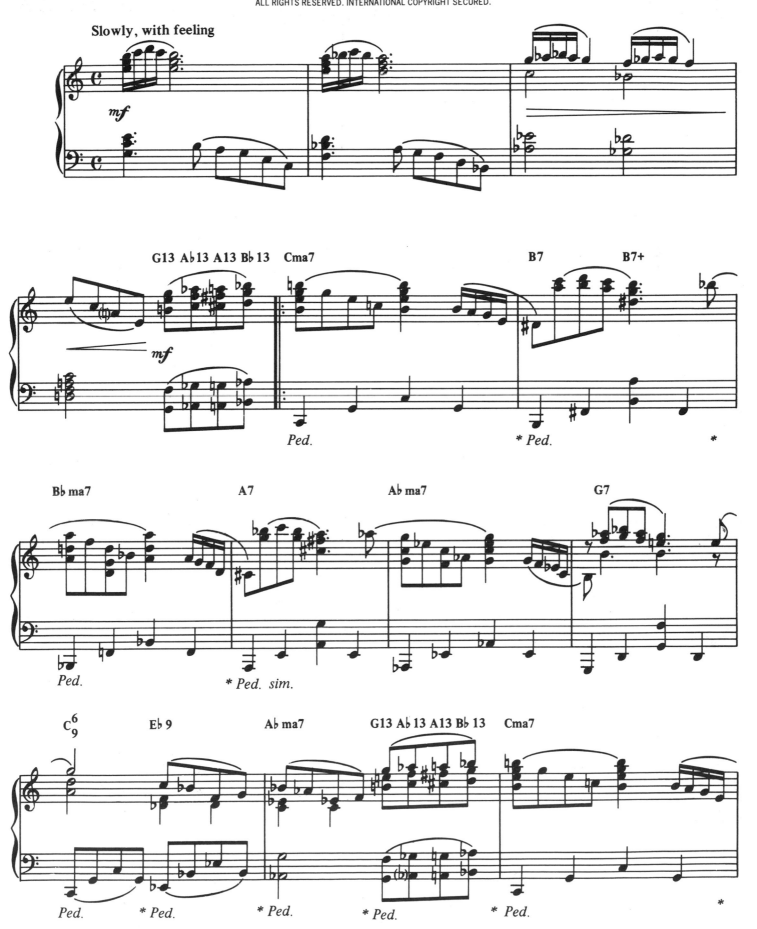

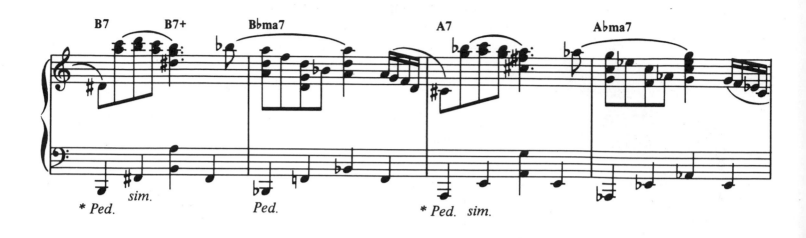

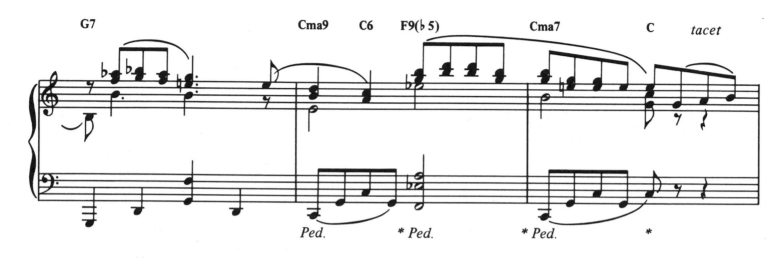

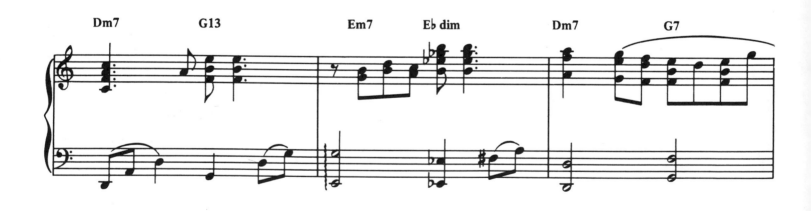

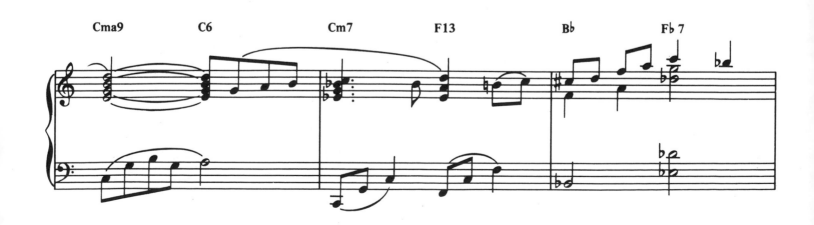

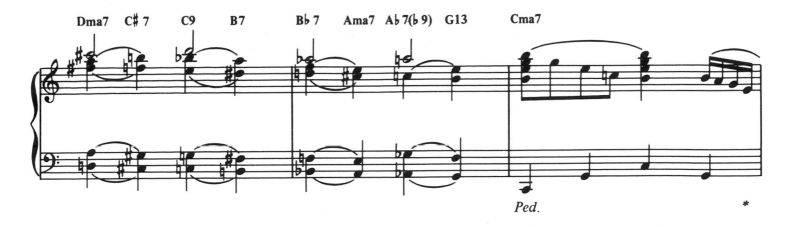

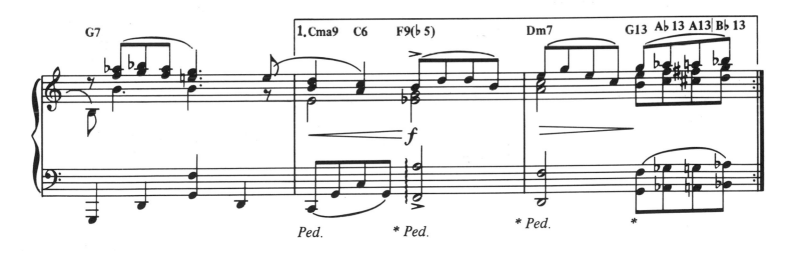

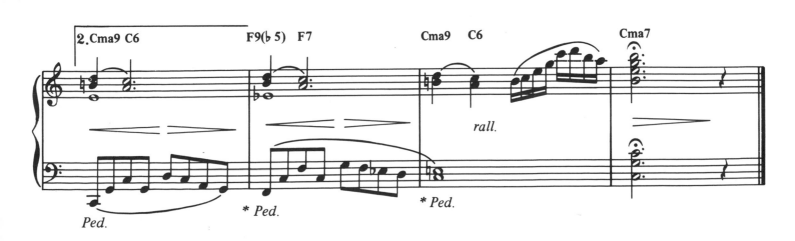

Fly Me To The Moon (In Other Words)

Words & Music by Bart Howard

Fools Rush In

Words by Johnny Mercer
Music by Rube Bloom

I'm Beginning To See The Light

Words & Music by Harry James, Duke Ellington, Johnny Hodges & Don George

23

24

I'm In The Mood For Love

Words & Music by Jimmy McHugh & Dorothy Fields

In Walked Bud

By Thelonious Monk

29

I'll Remember April

Words & Music by Don Raye, Gene de Paul & Patricia Johnson

Manteca

Words & Music by Dizzy Gillespie & Gil Fuller

One Note Samba (Samba De Uma Nota So)

Original Words by N. Mendonca. English Lyric by Jon Hendricks. Music by Antonio Carlos Jobim

B7(5♭)   Fm7   E7(♭5)

E♭maj7   A♭9   Dm7   D♭7   Cm7(sus4)

B7(5♭)   B♭6   tacet - - - - - - - - - - - - - - -*   E♭m7

A♭7   D♭maj7   D♭6   D♭maj7   D♭6

D♭m7   G♭7   Bmaj7   B6

Cm7(5b) B7(5b)   Dm7   Db7   Cm7(sus4)

B7(5b)   F+7   Dm7   Db7

Cm7   B7(5b)   Fm7

E7(b5)   Ebmaj7   Ab9   Db6

To Coda ⊕

(with a jazz feel)

C7   Bmaj7   Bb6

38

Round Midnight

By Cootie Williams & Thelonious Monk

42

Satin Doll

Words by Johnny Mercer
Music by Duke Ellington & Billy Strayhorn

Moderately, with a strong beat

Slightly Out Of Tune (Desafinado)

English Lyric by Jon Hendricks & Jessie Cavanaugh
Music by Antonio Carlos Jobim

Stormy Weather

Words by Ted Koehler
Music by Harold Arlen

Sophisticated Lady

Words by Irving Mills & Mitchell Parish
Music by Duke Ellington

Take Five

By Paul Desmond

Take The 'A' Train

Words & Music by Billy Strayhorn

These Foolish Things

Words by Eric Maschwitz
Music by Jack Strachey

Undecided

Words by Sid Robin
Music by Charles Shavers

Unforgettable

Words & Music by Irving Gordon

Wave

Words & Music by Antonio Carlos Jobim

Bbm7　Ebᵇ/Bb　tacet　　　*　Ebm7　　　　　　　Ab9/Gb

Fm7　　　　　　　　　　　　　　　　Dbm7/Gb

Gb9/Fb　　　　　　Ebm7　　　　　　　F7#5b9　　　　tacet　　　*

Bbmaj9　　　　　　Gbdim　　　　　　Fm7

Bb7(9b)　　　　　　Eb　　　　　　　Ebm6

71

A9 tacet   * Am7/D   D7   Ab7   G7

Cm7   F/C   Cm7   F/C   tacet   * Cm7   F/C   tacet   *

Fm7   Bb9/Ab   Gm7

Ebm7/Ab   Ab9/Gb

Fm7   G7#5b9   tacet   * Cmaj9

You've Changed

Words by Bill Carey
Music by Carl Fischer

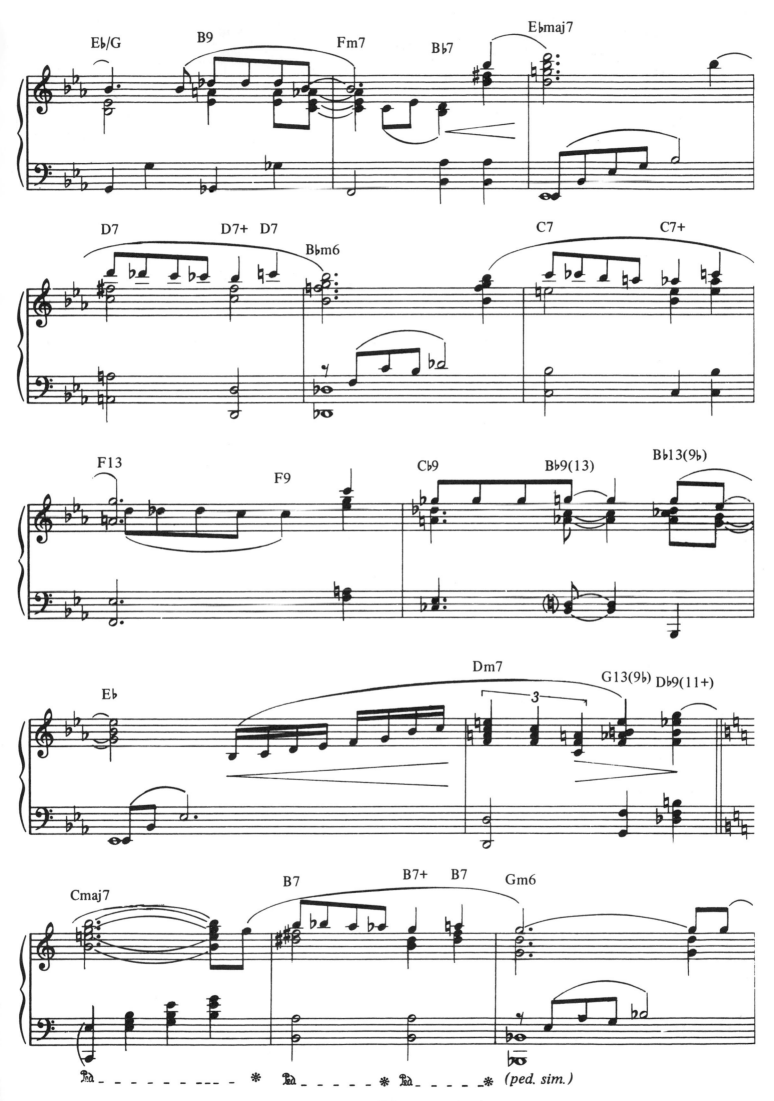